KING SOLOMON AND THE QUEEN OF SHEBA

Written by

BLU GREENBERG & LINDA TARRY

Illustrated by

AVI KATZ

PITSPOPANY

NEW YORK ◆ JERUSALEM

Dedication by Blu Greenberg

To my loves, Sacha, Keren, Itai, Yael, Noam, Joseph, Elliot, Emily, Jacob, Eran, Netanel, Eytan

Dedication by Linda Tarry

*God has truly blessed me with many loving friends — especially Dorothy Tananbaum
and Yaacov Peterseil, who conceived the idea for this book, which was written:*

In loving memory of my grandmother, "Mommie"

In honor of my parents, Hester James Anderson and Dorothy Lee Anderson

To my darling husband, Jim, and children, Victor and Kristen, who support me always

Special Acknowledgements

*The authors wish to express their gratitude to two special people, Yaacov Peterseil
and Dorothy Tananbaum, of Pitspopany Press. Not only did they conceive of the idea of this book,
but they graciously helped us through each stage of this work.
We also give special thanks to Lisa Weaver of Union Theological Seminary, to Barbara Gordon,
and to Barbara Black Koltuv who provided us with important research on the
Queen of Sheba. To Wendy Bernstein for her expert editing skills; to JJ Greenberg for his perfect
sense of nuance; to junior editors, "Krissy" Chard and Leah Hunt Hendrix,
who provided valuable editorial assistance; to Chaim Mazo for coordinating the technical
production; and to James R. Chard, the 24 hour computer expert.*

Published by Pitspopany Press
Text copyright © 1997 Blu Greenberg and Linda Tarry
Illustrations copyright © 1997 Avi Katz
Design by Benjie Herskowitz

PITSPOPANY PRESS books may be purchased for educational or special sales
by contacting: Marketing Director, Pitspopany Press, 40 East 78th Street,
New York, New York 10021. Fax: (212) 472-6253

ISBN: 0-943706-90-4
Printed in Hungary

CONTENTS

FOREWORD
by Blu Greenberg

When I was growing up, I read in my Bible the story of Solomon and Sheba. Few details were given, but still, I understood the Queen of Sheba to be an adventurous and bold queen, and Solomon to be the wisest of kings. These were exciting images to me, tucked away in my mind for some future encounter.

Then, in 1955, during the year that I spent in Israel, I visited an old family friend, Bessie Gotsfeld. Bessie was involved in helping to bring the first young Ethiopian Jews to Israel. Until then, I had not known that there were black Jews. Bessie explained that for thousands of years their ancestors had dreamed of coming to live in the land of Israel. These were the descendants of that king and queen of long ago.

Now fast-forward to the year 1991, to a real live miracle. In the midst of internal war, thousands of Ethiopian Jews were being airlifted to Israel, on planes that had been sent by the Israeli government. Somehow, it deepened the thrill to learn that the entire Jewish community was involved and that this project was called Operation Solomon.

To witness this miracle was one of the special religious moments of my life. What it said to me as a Jew was that color didn't matter, that black people were part of my Jewish family. On a larger canvas, this could also serve to bring Jews and blacks closer together.

Retelling a story now about the ancient connections between our two people seemed like a wonderful opportunity to continue that process. Writing this book with Linda Tarry, an African-American Christian woman, further symbolized for me those connections. As we worked together so joyfully and shared ideas, I also came to understand many things about her beliefs as a Christian and her values as an African-American woman.

A second reason for writing this book is that this is the story of a real and powerful queen, not just a make-believe one. Women and girls of all races, colors, and religions should have such models before them as they begin to make their own life choices.

The third reason is that this is a tale about monotheism, the belief in one God. Sometimes, people of our generation sometimes forget how revolutionary this idea is, or take it for granted, or worse, use religion to build barriers and make wars. But we learn from Solomon and Makeda how a religious belief can unite, not divide us.

Finally, I wanted to write this book for my grandchildren. I hope that they enjoy this story and learn from it, and I hope, dear reader, that you will, too.

FOREWORD
by Linda Tarry

For most of my adult life, I have been involved in activities that have brought together American Jews and African-Americans through a wide variety of social, religious and educational programs. As an example, I have been a docent at the Jewish Museum in New York City for an exhibit titled, "Bridges and Boundaries, the History of African American and American Jews."

It was therefore natural for me to be attracted to the ancient story of the link between King Solomon of Israel and Queen Makeda of Sheba; especially since the story is historically true and is told by Christians, Jews, and Muslims as part of their faith tradition. I saw retelling the story as a wondrous opportunity to show how two disparate cultures can learn from each other, and enrich each other.

Another reason for my fascination with this story is that the strength, enterprise and character of this great black queen provides a role model for young African-American women. It is important for young girls to know about powerful female personalities in the Bible who have demonstrated – through actions and deeds – their ability to rule entire nations, to achieve spiritual well-being, and to enjoy cultural and economic success.

The collaborative effort between Blu Greenberg (a white Jewish woman) and myself (a black Christian woman) to write this book is yet another way to view the legend of Solomon and Makeda and their ability to overcome differences. We have drawn upon our respective backgrounds to provide new depth and feeling to this ancient biblical story and give it a modern flavor.

I sincerely hope our efforts will provide young people of all backgrounds with both an exciting story of two historical young leaders, and an educational experience in multiculturalism and understanding differences between each of us.

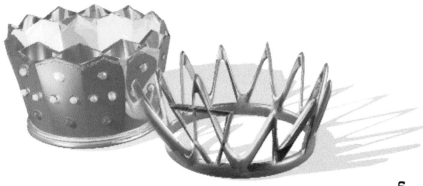

THE YOUNGEST RIDDLER

Long, long ago, in a land called Sheba, there lived a beautiful, young princess by the name of Makeda. She had big brown eyes and dark skin, and her thick black hair was woven into many braids.

Princess Makeda had two brothers, Prince Maru and Prince Seku. They included her in all of their games and adventures. When Makeda would return from the palace gardens with scraped knees, her mother, Queen Menalehush, would chide her, saying, "This is not exactly how a girl behaves." But Queen Menalehush always laughed when she said those words. So Makeda knew that her mother was really quite proud of her adventurous spirit.

Makeda was very kind. Although she was a princess, she would often

travel with her mother outside the gates of the palace to bring food and clothing to the poor families of the palace city.

Makeda was also very smart. She enjoyed trying to stump the palace elders with her questions. When she was only six years old, she composed her first riddle: "What continues to weigh the same no matter how big or how small it gets?" Makeda asked the king's wisest advisors, but none of them knew the answer. "A hole," she told them, laughing, "because a hole weighs nothing, no matter what size it is!"

A FATHER'S CHOICE

hen Makeda was 18 years old, her father, King Abera, became ill. The king said to his royal advisors, "I shall not live much longer. I must now begin to prepare for one of my children to take over the throne when I die. Everyone expects that I will choose Prince Maru, my eldest son. But there are things about him that trouble me. Maru is not always polite to others. Sometimes he throws temper tantrums. And he shows off in front of his friends.

"My second son, Seku, has no desire to be king. Instead, he loves to write poetry, listen to music and dream of faraway places. No, it cannot be Seku either. I must do what is best for my people.

"I will choose Makeda. The people love her. She is kind to everyone and she is also very wise."

The members of the royal court rejoiced. They said, "Princess Makeda will make a wonderful ruler."

Only Prince Maru protested. "Father, you cannot deny me the throne. It is my birthright, as I am the eldest son. Besides, Makeda is only a girl. She isn't fit to be the ruler. Father, please don't do this to me. I will be the laughing stock of the kingdom."

But King Abera knew what was best for the kingdom of Sheba. His decision was final.

A great coronation was planned. Everyone within the palace began to prepare. The tailors sewed a beautiful new gown for the princess. The musicians practiced on their drums and horns. The royal dancers perfected new movements. The court jesters made up new jokes. The palace was abuzz with excitement.

Throughout the land, people prepared gifts to bring to the new queen: chickens and wild geese, rare fruits and flowers, gold and silver — each person according to his or her own means.

But before the coronation could take place, King Abera became weaker. He realized that he would not live to place the crown on the head of his young daughter. He called Makeda to him to bid her farewell. "My child, you have inherited a good and rich land," he said to her. "Cherish it. Rule your people with kindness. As a mighty queen, do not forget that wisdom is more precious than all the gold and riches in the universe. Remember, follow wisdom wherever you find it." Then he closed his eyes for the last time.

Makeda wept at the thought that she would never again see her father. She would always remember her father's final words.

MAKEDA BECOMES QUEEN

he day of the coronation arrived. Over her beautiful new gown, Makeda wore the ancient royal robes of Sheba. A golden crown set with sparkling jewels was placed upon her head. All the people shouted, "Long live Makeda our queen!"

From the balcony of the palace, Makeda spoke to the great assembly gathered in the courtyard below. "Thank you for sharing this day with me, a day that I will never forget. I promise you that I will follow in my father's

path. Your voices will always be heard, and justice and peace will continue to reign in this land."

Queen Mother Menalehush, Prince Maru and Prince Seku were at her side. All were smiling, but Makeda could see the sadness in Maru's eyes. She felt sorry for him, but she knew that her father had picked her over her brothers, and that she had to carry out his wish.

And indeed, Queen Makeda ruled the land well. She encouraged the people to plant new spices. Sheba became an important center along the spice trade route. The port of Sheba was busy from morning until night. Ships came from many distant places. The men of Sheba built boats. The women cut precious stones and made necklaces and earrings. The old and young harvested spices. Donkeys and camels carried their loads to the ports.

KING SOLOMON THE WISE

In a land far away from Sheba, 100 days by camel and boat, there lived a king by the name of Solomon. Solomon had inherited the throne from his father, David, the greatest king of Israel.

Solomon was very wise. Even as a little boy, he showed a talent for settling disputes between people. When he was 11 years old, he helped his father, King David, settle an argument between a shepherd and a farmer.

One night, the shepherd's sheep entered the farmer's field and ate all his crops. The farmer was very angry at the shepherd. He said, "I have lost everything. You should have kept your sheep behind your fences and not let them run through my field. Now I'll have

nothing to sell in the marketplace. How will I feed my children?"

"It's not my fault that the sheep ate all of your crops," answered the shepherd. "*You* should have put up better fences."

They argued and argued. Finally, the matter was brought before King David. The king decided that it was the shepherd's fault for not watching his sheep. Therefore, the sheep should now be given to the farmer. After all, the sheep had eaten all the farmer's crops. The farmer was happy, but the shepherd cried, "Now, how will I feed *my* children? I will have no wool or milk to sell."

Young Solomon had an idea. "Father," he said, "the farmer lost his crops, but he still has his land. Next year he will be able to grow new crops. Let the farmer keep the sheep just for this year and sell their wool and milk. Next year, when the farmer's crops grow again, he should return the sheep to the shepherd."

King David said, "My son, that is very good advice. I will do as you say."

The farmer and the shepherd were both satisfied with this decision. Many years later, when Solomon became king, they came to his coronation as friends and reminded Solomon of the story.

SOLOMON BUILDS THE TEMPLE

Solomon loved God and he loved peace.

After he became king, Solomon said to his court advisors, "I want to build a great Temple to God. It was my father's dream to build this Temple but God did not choose him to do so."

"Why not?" asked the court advisors.

"Because my father was a warrior who fought in many battles," answered the king. "The Temple is supposed to be built in a time of peace, not war, so we must begin to build now."

King Solomon brought together architects and stone masons, wood carvers and gold artisans. They built a glorious Temple to God. Before long, people everywhere heard that Solomon's Temple in Jerusalem was the most magnificent building in the world.

In other ways, too, Solomon was a very successful king. He built

Israel into a great trading nation. When spice traders from Sheba returned home from their travels to the land of Israel, they brought back not only copper and honey, but also stories of the wise King Solomon and his great Temple.

Many of these stories were told to the Queen of Sheba by Tamarin, her chief advisor. The queen enjoyed hearing stories about Solomon. "He is so wise," she would say to Tamarin. "I would like to meet this great king one day."

"Perhaps, one day, you shall," Tamarin would answer.

The Hud Hud Bird

At the same time that Makeda was thinking of visiting King Solomon, Solomon was hearing stories about the land of Sheba. The king's merchants had traveled far and wide to bring back building materials for the Holy Temple. They also brought back reports of the beautiful land of Sheba, where peace and justice reigned.

"Who is the king that rules this wonderful land?" Solomon asked Eran, his most trusted advisor.

"There is no king, sire, but a queen. Her people say she rules with kindness and wisdom. And like you, my lord, she maintains peace in all her land."

"A queen!" exclaimed Solomon. "But has she no king?"

"No, your majesty, she is not married. Some say it is because she is so devoted to her people. And some say," Eran lowered his voice, "that she is a sorceress, a giant who towers over the tallest of men. Our spies say that she is part human and part animal, with the face and body of a woman but the feet of a goat."

"Well, I should like to see her for myself," Solomon told him. "Let us invite her to our land, to see the Temple of God."

Solomon was quiet for a moment. Then he asked, "Tell me, Eran, what god does she worship?"

"Her merchants worship a sun god," Eran answered. "I have heard that the queen and her court worship animals, trees and the moon as well."

"How long will it take for an invitation to reach the queen?" inquired Solomon.

"One hundred days by camel and boat, your majesty," Eran told the king. "But the seas are rough and we cannot begin a journey until the winter winds die down."

"I can't wait so long,"

declared the king. And then he asked a strange question. "Are there any birds that our merchants have brought back from the land of Sheba?"

"The hud hud bird," Eran answered. "It has a loud caw and a red beak."

"Bring one to me immediately," King Solomon commanded.

Next, Solomon called in Itai, his most skilled scribe. "Itai, write an invitation on the finest, most delicate parchment, light enough for a bird to carry."

When Itai finished, the invitation was attached to the hud hud bird's leg and the bird was set free. It flew high above the mountains and valleys, seas and deserts, as it journeyed home.

Queen Makeda Accepts An Invitation

One morning, as Queen Makeda sat on her throne, her ladies in waiting rushed in breathlessly. They carried a small scroll. "Dear queen, this was sent for you," they said excitedly. "It was tied to the leg of a hud hud bird, returning home from a faraway land."

The queen unraveled the scroll:

To the honorable Queen of Sheba,

I, King Solomon, son of David, King of Israel,

do hereby invite you to a feast

celebrating the completion of God's Temple.

I request that you come to the beautiful land of Israel.

Come to the city of holiness, Jerusalem,

Where we give honor to the One God of the Universe.

When Makeda finished reading the scroll, she announced to all the members of the royal court, "I shall go."

The people were upset when they heard that their queen was leaving. They feared that trouble might arise in their peaceful kingdom while she

was away. They were also worried about their queen's safety.

But Makeda reassured them, saying, "Prince Maru and Prince Seku will rule the land in my absence. Tamarin will help them as he has always helped me."

Nevertheless, the members of the court continued to question her. "Does not the land of Sheba have everything that you need? Why would you want to go to a faraway land?"

The queen answered, "Before my father died, he said to me, 'Follow wisdom wherever you find it.' From him I learned that wisdom is more precious than all the gold and silver in the world. I have heard of the great wisdom of King Solomon. I will go to him and bring back what I learn so I may share it with you."

Now the people understood why Queen Makeda wished to travel to King Solomon's land. "Go, your majesty, and our hearts go with you," they said.

When she was alone, Makeda thought to herself, I must test the king to see if he is as wise as they say he is. I shall make up the cleverest riddles to test the wisdom of Solomon.

There was much work to be done before the long journey. The caravans had to be organized. Decisions had to be made: Who would go with the queen and who would stay? What gifts to bring? How much water and food would be needed for the journey? Which was the best route?

Finally, all was ready. They sailed up the Nile River. Then they traveled by camel through mountains and deserts, plains and coast lands, until they came within sight of Jerusalem. It rose like a jewel in the mountains.

QUEEN MAKEDA MEETS KING SOLOMON

The city of Jerusalem was surrounded by stone walls on which Solomon's watchmen stood guard. Suddenly there was a commotion. "Look! A caravan is coming," shouted the guards when they saw the travelers below. "We must send a messenger to the king."

The messenger reached the king quickly. "A large caravan is coming," he reported. "The travelers come in friendship, for they are unarmed. We can tell it is a royal caravan by the beautiful silver and purple carriage that is being carried, but we do not know who is inside."

It must be the Queen of Sheba, thought the king. But could she have arrived so soon? I wasn't expecting her until next month. It is a good thing the special pool I built was completed yesterday. I shall use the pool to test if what they say about her strange feet is true.

To his servants he said, "Hurry! Go down the mountain and bring them to the palace."

The queen was brought directly to the chambers Solomon had

built for her. Although Solomon wished to see Queen Makeda immediately and she wished to see him, it was the custom to allow foreign visitors several days to rest after a long journey.

Finally, Queen Makeda was taken to see King Solomon. To reach his throne, she saw she would have to cross a shallow pool of water. Makeda realized at once that Solomon had been told that she might have goat's feet and this was how he would discover the truth.

How clever, she thought, as she removed her sandals and gently tucked up her skirt about her. A beautiful ankle dipped into the water.

Solomon, who had been watching her closely, breathed a sigh of relief.

"The tales you have been told about me are not true," Makeda smiled.

I can see that she is as clever as she is beautiful, Solomon said to himself.

After reaching his throne, Makeda presented King Solomon with an

emerald bracelet. Solomon marveled at the perfectly chiseled stones. "How talented are the artisans of Sheba. Thank you," he said to her.

Makeda also gave him an ebony sculpture in the likeness of a lion, the symbol of the sun god in the land of Sheba. In addition, she brought yards of wool and cotton; rolls of pure silk dyed in indigo; baskets of spices; and the wondrous pheremon, a perfume known only to the people of Sheba.

King Solomon also gave gifts to Queen Makeda: flax and honey, and a sapphire box filled with gold ornaments for her beautiful braids. He also presented her with an ivory sculpture in the likeness of a lion. In the land of Israel, the lion is a symbol of the kingdom of David and the throne of Solomon.

THE RIDDLES

he next day King Solomon held a banquet in the queen's honor. While they were eating, the King saw that Makeda was deep in thought. "My dear Queen of Sheba, tell me what is on your mind?" he asked.

Makeda hesitated. Solomon gazed at her and said, "I believe you wish to test my wisdom, that you want to ask me riddles."

Makeda did not lower her eyes but looked directly at Solomon. "Yes," she said, "I don't know how you knew what I was thinking, but I do have some riddles to ask you."

"Then let us begin," the king advised.

Makeda posed the first riddle:

"What land has seen the sun shine upon it for one day only?"

Solomon answered quickly, "It is the land beneath the waters of the Red Sea. For one day only, the waters of the sea were divided so that a nation could walk across to the other side."

"Correct," Makeda said, amazed. "But how could you possibly

know that? It is a tale that is told in my country."

Solomon explained. "Though people in many lands speak of the miracle of the parting of the waters, they do not know that this miracle happened to the Jewish people, my people.

"Many centuries ago, my ancestors were slaves in the land of Egypt. God told Moses to lead the Jewish slaves out of Egypt. God had Moses perform many miracles until Pharaoh, the king of Egypt, finally agreed to let the slaves go free.

"But after they left Egypt, Pharaoh changed his mind and ordered his army to go after them. The Egyptian army pursued them, right up to the Red Sea. The Jews were very frightened. Either way they were trapped. If they

they tried to escape Pharaoh's army by running into the sea, they would drown. If they just stood there, the soldiers would kill them.

"Then suddenly a miracle happened. God parted the waters of the Red Sea. The Jews walked across on dry land. Just as they reached the other side, the waters closed up again and their enemies, who had tried to follow them, drowned in the sea."

Makeda listened with great interest. "That is quite a story," she said, surprised to learn that the tale she had heard as a child in Sheba was actually the story of the Jewish people.

"Yes," agreed King Solomon, "it is a story we often retell. But now, what other riddles do you have for me?"

"It is said that you know a great deal about nature," Makeda began. "Do you see that tree trunk?" she asked, pointing to the sawed off section of a tree that her servants had just brought in. "Both ends look exactly the same, but one end faced down, toward the root of the tree, and the other faced its branches. Can you tell me which end is which?"

King Solomon picked up the tree trunk and threw it into the royal pool. "The end that faces the roots sinks," announced the king, "and the end that faced the branches floats above the water."

Hmm, Makeda thought, although he is a king, he knows the secrets of nature as well as any farmer on the land.

The queen clapped her hands. Fifty young children rushed in, all the same height, all dressed exactly alike in skirts and blouses. Even their hair was the same length.

"As you see, my king," Makeda explained, "these children are all dressed like girls. But only 25 are girls and 25 are boys. Without coming closer, and without hearing their voices, can you tell me which are the boys

and which the girls?"

Solomon called aside his servant, who returned immediately with spiced candies. From his throne, Solomon tossed handfuls of the sweets to the children. Twenty-five of them gathered the candies in their skirts; twenty-five raised their hands in the air to catch the candies.

"Those who raised their hands are the boys," Solomon declared, "for they are unaccustomed to using a skirt to catch things."

"Wonderful, King Solomon!" the Queen of Sheba cried. "Wonderful! Wonderful!" echoed all the people in the court.

Queen Makeda clapped her hands again. Her servants entered carrying fifty flowering plants.

"Only one of these plants is real," announced the queen. "The others are imitations produced by artisans in Sheba. Can you tell which is the real plant?"

Solomon leaned over and whispered something into the ear of his servant. Moments later, the servant returned with a small hummingbird cupped in his hands. The bird was released. In a matter of seconds, it fluttered near one of the plants, busily drawing out the sweet nectar from its flower.

"Aha, that is the real plant!" the king pointed as everyone clapped.

"Is there no limit to the wisdom of our king?" the people asked one another.

who is god

akeda asked many more riddles that day and Solomon answered them one by one.

When the last riddle had been answered, Queen Makeda said, "King Solomon, I did not believe all that I had heard about you, so I came to see for myself. But you are even wiser than I had imagined. You surely deserve the great wealth and success that you enjoy."

"Deserve?" the king exclaimed. "I do not *deserve* anything."

"Then how do you account for all of this?" she asked with a sweep of her arm.

"It is a gift from the One God of the Universe," King Solomon answered. "God created the heavens and the earth, the sun, the moon, the seas, the plants and animals and all living things

upon the earth. God is everywhere, in everything."

"Not so," Queen Makeda protested. "It is the sun god to whom we owe everything. The sun warms us. It lights our land by day and it shines upon the moon at night. We live only because the sun grows our food, our plants and our trees. Without the sun we would surely die.

"All can see our sun," she continued. "But you say god is everywhere. How can you worship a god you cannot see?"

Solomon could tell by her tone that this was not the moment to speak further about his God. "Let us speak of these matters another time," he suggested.

Makeda, too, was not in the mood for a debate. "As you wish," she agreed.

That night, as Makeda lay in bed, her mind returned to Solomon's words: "Deserve? It is not that I deserve anything. It is all from the One God..."

How strange, she thought, and how fascinating.

Abraham and God

When Queen Makeda met King Solomon the next day, she immediately said, "Solomon, tell me more about your God."

"How did you know what is on my mind?" he asked.

"Because it has been on my mind ever since I left you. I could barely sleep last night," she told him.

"Come with me to see the great Temple of Jerusalem. Perhaps it will help you to understand how our people see our God."

Makeda accompanied Solomon to the great Temple. It was the harvest season and the Temple was bustling with activity. Everywhere she looked, Makeda saw sacrifices being offered. She could smell the incense and see the smoke rising in the air. "We do the same in our land," she said, "but here there are no idols and no images of the gods. How can that be?"

"For us there are no idols, only the One God of the Universe," King Solomon explained.

"But where is your God?" she pressed, still wanting to see or touch something solid.

"My queen," King Solomon carefully answered, "While we cannot see our God, our God is everywhere — in every rock and in every grain of sand, in every breath of air we take. God is in you and in me.

It was God who revealed to me the answers to your riddles. And, it was God," said the king, looking into Makeda's beautiful brown eyes, "who brought you to me."

The queen thought for a long moment. Then she asked, "Have your people always believed in one God?"

"No," Solomon replied, "long ago the ancestors of my people worshiped many gods — the sun, the moon, the stars and even animal gods. But we came to realize that there is only one true powerful God, the One God of the Universe.

"There is a story about Abraham, the father of our people, that may help you better understand what I am saying.

"When Abraham was a young man, he worked in his father's idol shop. Terah, Abraham's father, had to leave the shop for a short while so he put his son in charge of the store. A woman came in with a bowl of grain. Here, she said to Abraham, put this grain before the idols. It is my gift to them. When she left the shop, Abraham took a stick and smashed all of the idols except for one. Then he put the stick in the hand of that one idol.

"When Terah returned, he shouted, Who did this terrible thing? Abraham replied, A woman came in and gave me food for the idols. Then one idol said, I want to eat first. The next idol said, No, I want to go first. Soon all the idols were fighting with one another, each one saying, It's my turn! It's my turn! Finally, this one idol took a stick and smashed all the others.

"What! Terah yelled, Do you take me for a fool? You know that these idols have no power.

"Father, said Abraham, listen to your own words. Why should anyone worship these idols? There is only one powerful and true God.

"So Abraham packed his knapsack" concluded the king, "and left his father's house. He traveled far, and one day he heard the voice of the One God of the Universe. God told Abraham that he was right not to believe in idols, and that God and Abraham would be partners forever."

When Solomon finished his story, Makeda was deep in thought. "How strange that your God is everywhere and rules everything," she said. "Tell me more, Solomon."

Solomon then explained to her how God had not only taken the slaves out of Egypt and made them free, but had also given them the Torah as they journeyed through the Sinai Desert. Finally, after 40 years of wandering through the desert, God had brought the Jewish people to the land of Israel.

"In the Torah are the Ten Commandments and all the laws about justice and how to treat other people," the king added. "The Torah is the story of the covenant — the agreement — that God made with Abraham. This covenant was also made with Abraham's children and then again with Moses and the Jewish people. It is renewed with each generation."

Queen Makeda listened with great interest. "Solomon, I am beginning to understand," she said, "but I need more time to think about all of this."

THE QUEEN FOLLOWS WISDOM

hat night, as Makeda slept, her father appeared to her in a dream.

"Follow wisdom, my child," he commanded her. "Follow wisdom wherever you find it."

When she awoke, she knew that Solomon had given her the greatest gift of all — his wisdom about God and the universe. She understood that his words about God were more important than the answers to all the riddles in the world.

Suddenly, Makeda felt lonely and wanted to return to Sheba. Yet, as she thought about leaving Solomon, she felt sad.

But a choice had to be made.

When they saw each other again, Makeda said to Solomon, "It is time for me to return home. I must share with the people of Sheba the lessons I have learned from you."

Solomon looked sorrowful. He said, "Please, Makeda, do not leave me. You have become so precious to me. Stay by my side forever."

And then his voice softened, "Will you marry me?" he asked.

Makeda was surprised, thrilled and confused, all at once. She did not know what to do. Should she stay and marry Solomon, or return to Sheba? No matter how deep her love for Solomon, she knew the people of Sheba also needed her.

At last she answered, "I will marry you, for I love you and wish to be in your heart always. But I must return home to Sheba before too long."

A GREAT WEDDING

A great wedding was planned. The celebration lasted for weeks. King Solomon and Queen Makeda spent many happy days together. But they realized that eventually their time together would come to an end.

After several months, Makeda said to Solomon, "I must keep my promise and return to Sheba." She began to prepare for the long journey home.

On the eve of her departure, Solomon's heart was heavy. He came to her chambers laden with gifts. Among them was a gold ring, set with diamonds and rubies. On the inside of the ring, Solomon had engraved these words:

Place me as a seal upon your heart

Makeda slipped the ring on her finger and said, "I will keep this forever, as a sign of our love. Do not be sad, dear Solomon," she told him, though she felt quite sad herself, "We will see each other again some day."

Queen Makeda did not tell King Solomon what she suspected — that she was carrying his child. It was too soon to know for sure, and if she waited to tell him, it would be even more difficult to leave.

THE JOURNEY HOME

After a long journey, Makeda reached the land of Sheba. The people came out to greet her with great joy and thanksgiving, for they were happy to have their beloved Queen home at last.

Soon after her return to the palace, Makeda gave birth to a baby boy. She named him Ben LeHaham, which in Hebrew means, son of the wise. The Queen Mother Menalehush loved her little grandson and called him Menelik. The boy was adored by all in the palace and beyond. Everyone knew that one day he would inherit the throne.

Soon after the birth of Ben LeHaham-Menelik, Makeda began to share with everyone all she had learned while she was away. They were eager to hear everything she had to say about King Solomon, the people of Israel and the One God of the Universe.

When Ben LeHaham-Menelik reached the age of 13, Queen Makeda said to him, "My son, it is now time for you to visit your father. Go to him and tell him all that we have done in the land of Sheba. Tell him that now we, too, worship the One God of the Universe. Tell him that I love him and think of him every day."

"But mother, how will he know that I am his son?" the boy asked.

"You have his spark of wisdom. Besides," Makeda held up a mirror to the handsome face of her son, "this is exactly how he looks. He will recognize you immediately."

Once again the people of Sheba prepared for a great journey as the young son of Queen Makeda set off to meet his father....

THE END

AFTERWORD

by Barbara Ribakove Gordon

Prince Menelik stayed with his father, King Solomon, until he had learned all that King Solomon could teach him about being a ruler. When Menelik finally went home to Sheba, King Solomon sent with him an amazing gift: 12,000 of his own people – 1,000 from each of the Twelve Tribes of Israel – to help Menelik rule and to help his people continue the worship of God. Eventually, the people of Sheba stopped worshiping the sun god.

After the death of his beloved mother, Queen Makeda, Prince Menelik was crowned Emperor Menelik. He and his descendants ruled the land of Sheba wisely and well for many generations. By then, the religion of the country was called, Judaism. Even the name of the country had changed, from Sheba to Ethiopia.

As the years passed, however, new religions were introduced into the country, and many of the people converted to these new religions. Before long, there were wars between those who converted to the new religion and those who still worshiped in the way of King Solomon and Queen Makeda. In the end, the Jews were driven away from their cities and farms, into high and stony mountains. They became metalworkers and potters – trades other Ethiopians looked down on. A large number of them became sharecroppers, farming someone else's land in return for a small part of the crops. They were very poor, and their children were hungry.

But they always had the same dream as their ancestor, Queen Makeda – to go to Jerusalem. Every Jewish mother told her children, "Some day, you will go to Jerusalem, just like the queen."

Many years passed before their dream came true. King Solomon's country, Israel, was re-established, and its capital was exactly where King Solomon's capital had been – in Jerusalem!

You might think that all the Ethiopian Jews would have left at once for Jerusalem. But a cruel Communist government threw out the last ruler of Emperor Menelik's line, and wouldn't let anyone leave Ethiopia. Anyone who wanted to go to Jerusalem (or anywhere else) had to sneak away at night, through jungles, across rivers, over mountains and into deserts. Some died of exhaustion, hunger, thirst or disease.

But still, the Jews kept trying to reach Jerusalem. Other Jews from America helped them. And those who managed to escape from Ethiopia hid until brave secret agents from the new State of Israel could find them and take them to Jerusalem.

How did they go? Some crossed the Red Sea by boat as Queen Makeda had. Others flew in airplanes the queen never dreamed of. In Operation Moses, the Israelis, with help from the government of the United States, flew more than 8,000 Ethiopian Jews to Israel in just a few weeks time.

Most amazing of all, in 1991, more than 14,000 Ethiopian Jews were airlifted out of the Ethiopian capital, Addis Ababa, in just one day. That airlift was called Operation Solomon!

Today, practically all Ethiopian Jews live in Israel. It is hard for the older people to adjust to the big change from their little mountain villages in Ethiopia to the big modern cities in Israel. But they are glad to be in the homeland of their ancestors, and proud to see their children going to school and becoming teachers, doctors, engineers and scientists, living in freedom and dignity. Their lives have changed a lot.

But one thing will never change. Ethiopian mothers and fathers will always tell their children about how their people first came to be; how the great Queen Makeda and the famous King Solomon met, how the beautiful queen tested the wise king, how they loved each other – and how they knew that even though they had to part, some day in the future their children would come home.

And so they have.

Barbara Ribakove Gordon
Director, North American Conference of Ethiopian Jewry
165 East 56 Street, New York, NY 10022

The Land Of My Dreams

My name is Natan Kebede. I was born in 1971 in a small village called Mooly, in Ethiopia. I have 10 brothers and sisters. Ever since I was born, I had heard about the special place, Jerusalem, in the land of Israel, and dreamed of going there.

During the summer of 1980, about 400 people from our village set out to go to Israel. I was eight years old at the time. Since the Ethiopian government wouldn't let us leave, we had to figure out ways to sneak across the border. We all knew that there would be many dangers. The village elders decided that we should go to the Sudan border.

We always traveled at night and slept in trees during the day because we were afraid that someone might see us.

For three long weeks we walked in the desert. It was boiling hot during the day and cold at night. We never had enough food and we were always thirsty. Three separate times we were attacked by bandits who tried to steal what little clothing we had. It was a great miracle that no one was killed.

When we finally entered the Sudan, the Israeli Mosad agents found us and made us understand that they would help us get to Israel. We could not give up, they said. But some of us wanted to return to Ethiopia. I asked my father if the Israeli agents were Jews. I had never seen a white Jew before.

We waited one whole year until the Israelis told us it was our turn to go. We set out in trucks and traveled for two days to get to the sea. There, we were met by an Israeli commando unit, and they put us on a boat – we were going to Israel!

I could not believe that I would finally see the land of my dreams, the land my people had spoken about for thousands of years.

When we landed, it was as though we had just received the holy Torah. We bent down and kissed the ground of Israel, unable to stop our tears.

Today I feel like an Ethiopian Jew who has come home. The Israeli government has helped my people become part of the land. But for me, my greatest moment, next to coming here, was joining the army and serving in a combat unit. To be able to defend the country of your dreams is a wonderful thing. I am working now to help others realize their dreams, as God has helped me realize mine.